Anti Inflamn

MW01490604

50 Slow Cooker Recipes With Anti Inflammatory Ingredients

Great For Gout Relief!

Kate Marsh

These recipes are not intended to be any type of Medical advice. ALL individuals must consult their Doctors first and should always receive their meal plans from a qualified practitioner. These recipes are not intended to heal, or cure anyone from any kind of illness, or disease.

Please take not that these recipes are from the kitchen, and home of Kate Marsh, who's husband suffers from gout, and other forms of inflammation. She is only sharing her recipes based on her knowledge, and experience with cooking for inflammation relief. These recipes are not intended to cure anyone from their inflammation. Thank you, and enjoy!

Table of Contents

Pulled Chicken

Pumpkin Chicken Chili

Cream Cheese Chicken

Ratatouille with Chickpeas

Slow Cooked Chicken Fajitas

Wild Duck Breast L'Orange

Slow Roasted Herb Potatoes

Summer Squash Casserole

Caribbean Sweet Potato Stew

Slow Cooked Scalloped Potatoes

Black Bean Soup

Honey Sriracha Chicken Wings

Corn and Potato Chowder

Slow Cooked French Onion Soup

Slow Cooker Roasted Vegetables

Wild Duck Gumbo

Buffalo Chicken Pasta

Crock Pot Minestrone Soup

Lentil Cauliflower Stew

Crock Pot Lasagna

Slow Cooked Spinach Manicotti

Slow Cooked Mac and Cheese

Italian Vegetable and Pasta Soup

Pesto Chicken Sandwiches

Mushroom Risotto with Peas

Chicken Osso Buco

Warm Eggplant and Kale Panzanella

Slow Cooker Ribollita

Italian Wedding Soup

Penne with Tomato-Eggplant Sauce

Beef and Carrot Ragu

Italian Pork and Sweet Potatoes

Spaghetti with Sauce Italiano

Saucy Ravioli with Meatballs

Caponata Sicilianata

Italian Braised Chicken with Fennel and Cannellini

Char Siu Pork Roast

Mediterranean Roast Turkey

Vegetable and Chickpea Curry

Provençal Beef Daube

Smoky Slow Cooker Chili

Provençale Chicken

Pesto Lasagna with Spinach and Mushrooms

Curried Beef Short Ribs

Barley Stuffed Cabbage Rolls

Spinach Artichoke Dip

Creole Red Beans and Rice

White Bean Cassoulet

Loaded Baked Potatoes

Chicken with Carrots and Potatoes

Thank You!

Pulled Chicken

Ingredients:

3 Chicken Breasts – Boneless, Skinless

10 ½ Ounces of Condensed Tomato Soup

8 Ounces of Onion

¼ Cup of Vinegar

3 Tablespoon of Brown Sugar

1 Tablespoon of Worcestershire Sauce

½ Teaspoon of Salt

¼ Teaspoon of Dried Basil

1 Pinch of Ground Thyme

Hamburger Bun

Instructions:

Layer the chicken on the bottom of your Crock Pot.

Combine all of the other ingredients in a medium bowl and pour over the chicken.

Cover it tightly, and then cook it on low setting for 4-5 hours.

Remove the chicken, and then shred it using forks.

Return the chicken to your Crock Pot and cook it for about 1-2 hours.

Serve it on hamburger buns.

Nutritional Information:

Calories: 110

Total Fat: 4 1/2g

Saturated Fat: 1 1/2g

Carbohydrates: 9g

Protein: 9g

Pumpkin Chicken Chili

Ingredients:

1 Pound of Ground Chicken

1 Can of Chili Beans

1 Can of Black Beans

2 Cups of Cubed Pumpkin

1 Can of Tomatoes - Diced

1 Cup of Chopped Onion

3 Tablespoon of Brown Sugar

1 Tablespoon of Pumpkin Pie Spice

1 Tablespoon of Chili Powder

1 Tablespoon of Olive Oil

Instructions:

Heat the oil in a large pot on medium heat; brown the chicken, stir it often, until crumbly and not pink, approximately 10 minutes. Drain the chicken and discard the fat.

Transfer the chicken to your slow cooker. Stir in the diced pumpkin, chili beans, tomatoes, black beans, brown sugar, pumpkin pie spice, as well as the chili powder. Cook it on the low setting for 3 hours.

Nutritional Information:

Calories: 338

Total Fat: 9g

Saturated Fat: 0g

Carbohydrates: 41g

Protein: 25g

Cream Cheese Chicken

Ingredients:

3 lbs of Chicken Breast – Boneless, Skinless

1 Package of Italian Salad Dressing Mix

4 Tablespoons of Melted Butter

1 Small Onion - Chopped

1 Clove of Garlic- Chopped

1 Can of Cream of Chicken Soup

8 Ounces of Low Fat Cream Cheese

½ Cup of Chicken Broth

Instructions:

Place your chicken in your crock-pot, and then sprinkle the Italian seasoning on the chicken. Sprinkle it with 2 tablespoons of melted butter.

Cook it on the low setting for 4-6 hours.

Melt 2 tablespoons of butter in a pan, and then sauté the onions and the garlic. Add the Cream of Chicken Soup, the low fat cream cheese, as well as the chicken broth. Stir it until it is smooth.

Add the mix to your crock-pot. Cook on the low setting for an added hour.

Nutritional Information:

Calories: 547

Total Fat: 44g

Saturated Fat: 19g

Carbohydrates: 6g

Protein: 29g

Ratatouille with Chickpeas

Ingredients:

1 Tablespoon of Vegetable Oil

1 Onion - Chopped

4 Garlic Cloves - Minced

6 Cup of Eggplants - Cubed

2 Teaspoons of Basil

1 Teaspoon of Oregano

$1/2$ Teaspoons of Salt

$1/2$ Teaspoons of pepper

1 Red Bell Pepper

1 Yellow Bell Pepper

2 Zucchinis

$1/3$ Cups of Tomato Paste

1 Can of Chickpeas- Drained, Rinsed

1 Can of Tomatoes

$1/4$ Cup of Fresh Basil Chopped

Instructions:

In a large pan, heat the oil on medium, cook your onions, the garlic, the eggplant, the basil, oregano, and the salt and pepper, stirring sporadically until the onion is softened, approximately 10 minutes. Put it into the crockpot.

Halve, core, and then seed the peppers; cut them into 1-inch pieces. Cut the zucchini into halves lengthwise, and then cut them crosswise into 1 1/2-inch pieces. Add it to the crockpot.

Add tomato paste, chickpeas, and tomatoes, breaking up tomatoes with a spoon. Cover and cook on low for 4 hours, or until vegetables are tender. Stir in basil.

Nutritional Information:

Calories: 219

Total Fat: 37g

Saturated Fat: 1g

Carbohydrates: 40g

Protein: 9g

Slow Cooked Chicken Fajitas

Ingredients:

1 Red Bell Pepper

1 Yellow Bell Pepper

1 Green Bell Pepper

1 Onion

1 Packet Taco or Fajita Seasoning

1 Pound of Chicken Breasts – Boneless, Skinless

½ Cup of Chicken Broth

Toppings (Low Fat Cheese, Low Fat Sour Cream, or Salsa)

Tortillas

Instructions:

Slice the bell peppers and the onions in ¼ inch pieces. Add them to the bottom of your Crockpot.

Sprinkle the taco or fajita seasoning on the bell peppers and the onions in your Crockpot. Add in the chicken breasts and the chicken broth.

Cook it on the low setting for 6-8 hours.

Remove the chicken from the Crockpot and let cool slightly. Use two forks to shred the chicken. Add shredded chicken back to Crockpot and mix with peppers and onions.

Serve over tortillas or alone with your choice of toppings (like cheese, salsa, guacamole, sour cream, fresh cilantro).

Nutritional Information:

Calories: 235

Total Fat: 12g

Saturated Fat: 7g

Carbohydrates: 41g

Protein: 19g

Wild Duck Breast L'Orange

Ingredients:

2 Whole Wild Duck Breasts – Halved, Skin Removed

1/2 Teaspoons of Salt

1/4 Teaspoon of Black Pepper

2 Small Oranges – Peeled, Cut into 1/2-inch Pieces

1 Medium Apple - Cut into 1/2-inch pieces

1 Medium Onion - Cut into Eighths

1 Can (6 Ounces) Frozen Orange Juice Concentrate - Thawed

Instructions:

Sprinkle the duck with salt and pepper. Layer the duck, the oranges, the apples and the onions in a 3 1/2 - 6 quart slow cooker. Pour the orange juice concentrate on the top. Cover it and cook it on the low setting for 8-10 hours. Remove the duck from cooker and discard the fruit and the onion mixture.

Nutritional Information:

Calories: 206

Total Fat: 4g

Saturated Fat: 1g

Carbohydrates: 32g

Protein: 13g

Slow Roasted Herb Potatoes

Ingredients:

6 Medium potatoes

$1/4$ Cups of Water

1 Teaspoon of Salt

1 Teaspoon of Pepper

1 Teaspoon of Garlic Powder

1 Teaspoon of Minced Onion

$1/2$ Teaspoons of Dried Dill

1 Teaspoon of Italian Seasoning

1 Teaspoon of Parsley

4 Tablespoon of Butter

Instructions:

Chop your potatoes into half-moons (slice the potatos in half the long-ways, then to pieces). Place them into the crock-pot.

Add the water and then sprinkle it with all the herbs and the seasoning. Stir it to distribute the herbs evenly.

Add the butter into separate pieces on the top of your potatoes.

Cover it and cook it on the low setting for 5 hours.

Nutritional Information:

Calories: 353

Total Fat: 11g

Saturated Fat: 7g

Carbohydrates: 57g

Protein: 7g

Summer Squash Casserole

Ingredients:

9 Cup of Sliced Yellow Summer Squash (5 Medium Squashes)

1 Medium Onion - Chopped

1 Tablespoon of Butter

2 Cups of French Bread Crumbs

8 Ounces of Shredded Sharp Cheddar Cheese

2/3 Cups of Low Fat Sour Cream

½ Teaspoon of Garlic Salt

¼ Teaspoon of Pepper

1 Can (10 3/4 oz) Condensed Cream of Chicken Soup

1 Tablespoon of Butter - Melted

Chopped Fresh Parsley

Instructions:

Spray a 5- to 6-quart slow cooker. In a large microwavable bowl, microwave the squash, the onion, and 1 tablespoon of butter (uncovered) on the High setting for 10 minutes. Drain it.

In your slow cooker, mix in the squash mixture, 8 ounces of the breadcrumbs, and 1/2 cup of the cheese, the low fat sour cream, the garlic salt, the pepper and the soup. In small bowl, mix remaining 8 ounces of breadcrumbs, remaining 1/2 cup of cheese and the melted butter. Sprinkle the crumb mixture over squash. Cover it and then cook it on the low setting for 2 hours. Uncover it and remove the insert from your slow cooker. Let it stand for 30 minutes before serving. Sprinkle with parsley, if desired.

Nutritional Information:

Calories: 180

Total Fat: 12g

Saturated Fat: 6g

Carbohydrates: 12g

Protein: 5g

Caribbean Sweet Potato Stew

Ingredients:

2 Medium Sweet Potatoes

2 Chicken Breast Halves - Boneless

1 Pound of Chorizo Sausage

1 Large Onion - Chopped

2 Cloves of Garlic - Finely Minced

1 Can of Whole Tomatoes with Juice

1 Can of Garbanzo Beans - Drained

1 Teaspoon of Paprika

1 Teaspoon of Salt

1 Teaspoon of Thyme

1 Teaspoon of Ground Black Pepper

1/2 Teaspoons of Allspice

1/2 Teaspoons of Cumin

2 Tablespoons of Tomato Paste

Chopped Parsley

Instructions:

Peel and then dice the sweet potatoes into 1-inch cubes. Cut the chicken and the sausage into 1-inch pieces.

In your crock-pot, combine the sweet potatoes, your chicken, onion, sausage, garlic, tomatoes, paprika, beans, pepper, thyme, salt, allspice, the cumin, and the tomato paste. Cover it and allow it to simmer on the low setting until the sweet potatoes are tender, approximately 4 hours.

To serve it ladle it into bowls and garnish it with parsley.

Nutritional Information:
Calories: 396
Total Fat: 40g
Saturated Fat: 3g
Carbohydrates: 30g
Protein: 30g

Slow Cooked Scalloped Potatoes

Ingredients:

3 Pounds of Yukon Gold Potatoes – Unpeeled, Thinly Sliced

1 Large Onion - Thinly Sliced

1 Can of Campbell Condensed Cheddar Cheese Soup

1/2 Cups of Milk

1/2 Cups of Parmesan Cheese

1/2 Teaspoons of Salt

1/4 Teaspoon of Black Pepper

8 Ounces of Shredded Cheddar Cheese

Directions:

Spray your 6-quart slow cooker with cooking spray. Layer 1/3 of your potatoes and ½ of the onions in your cooker. Repeat layers. Top it with the rest of the potatoes.

Stir in the soup, milk, Parmesan, salt, and the black pepper in a bowl. Pour the soup mix on the potatoes. Cover it and cook it on the high setting for 4-5 hours.

Sprinkle it with Cheddar cheese. Cover it and allow it to stand for 5 minutes.

Nutritional Information:

Calories: 330

Total Fat: 11g

Saturated Fat: 6g

Carbohydrates: 46g

Protein: 12g

Black Bean Soup

Ingredients:

2 Cloves of Garlic

1 Medium Onion

2 Stalks of Celery

2 Medium Carrots

1 lb. of Black Beans - Uncooked

8 Ounces of Salsa

1 Tablespoon of Chili Powder

½ Tablespoon of Cumin

1 Tablespoon of Oregano

4 Cups of Vegetable Broth

2 Cups of Water

Instructions:

Mince the garlic, dice the onions, as well as the celery. Grate your carrots on a large cheese grater. Rinse the black beans using a colander under cold water and pick out any debris.

Combine the garlic, your onion, the celery, black beans, carrots, salsa, chili powder, oregano, cumin, the vegetable broth, and the water in your 5-7 quart cooker. Stir it well.

Place the lid on your slow cooker and then cook it on the high setting for 6-8 hours. Once the beans are soft, blend in the soup until it's thick.

Nutritional Information:

Calories: 114

Total Fat: 1g

Saturated Fat: 1g

Carbohydrates: 19g

Protein: 6g

Honey Sriracha Chicken Wings

Ingredients:

4 Pounds of Chicken Wings - Frozen

3/4 Cups of Sriracha Sauce

3/4 Cups of Honey

2 Tablespoons of Unsalted Butter

Juice of One Lime

Instructions:

Add the sriracha, honey, butter, and lime juice. Stir in to combine. Add in the chicken wings. Stir it until the wings are well coated. Cook them on the low setting for 6-8 hours or on the high setting for 3-4 hours.

Remove the wings from your slow cooker and then place them on a baking sheet that is lined with foil. Drizzle on the sauce from the cooker on the wings.

Set your oven to broil. Place the baking sheet inside the oven and bake them for 2-3 minutes. Remove them from the oven.

Nutritional Information:

Calories: 321

Total Fat: 10g

Saturated Fat: 2g

Carbohydrates: 19g

Protein: 35g

Corn and Potato Chowder

Ingredients:

24 Ounces of Red Potatoes - Diced

1 (16-ounce) Package of Frozen Corn

3 Tablespoon of Flour

6 Cups of Chicken Stock

1 Teaspoon of Dried Thyme

1 Teaspoon of Dried Oregano

1/2 Teaspoons of Garlic Powder

1/2 Teaspoons of Onion Powder

Salt and Black Pepper

2 Tablespoons of Unsalted Butter

1/4 Cups of Heavy Cream

Instructions:

Place the potatoes and the corn into your slow cooker. Stir in the flour and toss it to combine it. Stir in the chicken stock, the thyme, garlic powder, oregano, onion powder, salt and pepper.

Cover it and cook it on the low setting for 7-8 hours or high heat for 3-4 hours. Stir in the butter and the heavy cream.

Serve it immediately.

Nutritional Information:

Calories: 384

Total Fat: 144g

Saturated Fat: 5g

Carbohydrates: 54g

Protein: 9g

Slow Cooked French Onion Soup

Ingredients:

1/4 Cups of Butter

6 Thyme Sprigs

1 Bay Leaf

5 Pounds of Sweet Onions - Vertically Sliced

1 Tablespoon of Sugar

6 Cups of Beef Stock

2 Tablespoons of Red Wine Vinegar

1 1/2 Teaspoons of Salt

1 Teaspoon of Black Pepper

24 Slices Whole-Grain French Bread

5 Ounces of Gruyère Cheese - Shredded

Instructions:

1. Place the butter, thyme, and the bay leaf in the bottom of your 6-quart slow cooker. Add in the onions, and then sprinkle it with sugar. Cover it and cook then cook it on the high setting for 8 hours.

2. Remove the thyme and the bay leaf; discard it. Add in the stock, vinegar, the salt, and some pepper; cook it covered on the high setting for 30 minutes.

3. Preheat your broiler to high.

4. Arrange the bread in a single layer; broil it for 30 seconds on each side. Place 8 ounces of soup on each of the12 ramekins or ovenproof bowls. Top each serving with 2 slices and 2 tablespoons of cheese. Place the 6 ramekins on a jelly-roll pan; broil it for 2 minutes or until cheese melts. Repeat the procedure with the remaining 6 ramekins, slices, and the cheese.

Nutritional Information:

Calories: 240

Total Fat: 8g

Saturated Fat: 3g

Carbohydrates: 33g

Protein: 9g

Slow Cooker Roasted Vegetables

Ingredients:

4 Potatoes – Chopped, Large Pieces

2 Carrots

1/2 Onion - Sliced

2 Zucchinis - Thickly Sliced

Olive Oil

1 Packet of Dry Italian Dressing Mix

Instructions:

Place the chopped vegetables in a bowl

Drizzle the vegetables with the olive oil.

Sprinkle the packet of Italian seasoning on the vegetables.

Lightly toss it so all of the vegetables are covered in oil and the seasoning.

Spray the slow cooker with non-stick spray and dump the seasoned vegetables in.

Cook it on the low setting for 5-7 hours or on the high setting for 3-4 hours.

Nutritional Information:

Calories: 93

Total Fat: 5g

Saturated Fat: 1g

Carbohydrates: 12g

Protein: 3g

Wild Duck Gumbo

Ingredients:

1 Duck

1 lb of Smoked Pork Sausage

$1/2$ Cups of Vegetable Oil

8 Ounces of Chopped Onion

8 Ounces of Chopped Bell Pepper

8 Ounces of Chopped Onion Tops

$1/4$ Cups of Parsley

2 Teaspoons of Salt

1 Teaspoon of Pepper

Instructions:

Cut up your duck and season it with salt and pepper.

Pour the cooking oil into a large black iron pot. Heat the oil and add in the cut up duck.

Brown all sides of the meat, gradually add in a small amounts of water to keep it from burning.

When it is browned, remove the meat and then pour off the excess oil. Return the meat to the pot and then add in enough water to cover your meat.

Cut up the sausage in to thick slices and then add it to the pot.

Add all of the vegetables and extra salt and pepper.

Simmer it until the meat is very tender. Keep adding in the water as the sauce cooks down to keep up the level.

Turn the gumbo off for a bit so that excess grease or oil will rise to the top, skim it off.

Serve in a bowl over rive or plain.

Nutritional Information:

Calories: 435

Total Fat: 23g

Saturated Fat: 12g

Carbohydrates: 21g

Protein: 19g

Buffalo Chicken Pasta

Ingredients:

1 - 1½ Pounds of Chicken – Boneless, Skinless

3 Cups of Chicken Broth

½ Cup of Buffalo Wing Sauce

1 Tablespoon of Ranch Dressing Mix

½ Teaspoon of Garlic Powder

¼ Teaspoon of Celery Salt

¼ Teaspoon of Salt

⅛ Teaspoon of Pepper

8 Ounces of Cream Cheese

8 Ounces of Shredded Sharp Cheddar

1 Tablespoon of Corn Starch

1 Tablespoon of Water

16 Ounce of Linguine Noodles

Chopped Cilantro for Garnish

Instructions:

Place the chicken, the broth, ¼ cup of buffalo wing sauce, and the seasonings in a crock-pot.

Top it with cream cheese and some shredded cheese

Cover it and cook it on the high setting for 4 hours or low for 8 hours.

When the chicken is completely cooked; remove it to a separate bowl and then shred it using two forks.

Add in the remaining ¼ cup of buffalo wing sauce to the chicken and then toss it to coat it well.

Set it aside.

Whisk together the cornstarch and the water. Add it to the crock-pot.

Use a whisk to stir it until the cheese and the cream cheese is combined and completely smooth.

Break the noodles in half and then place it in the crock-pot.

Top it with chicken and then cover it.

Turn the crock-pot on high for 40-60 minutes, stir it 3-4 times while it is cooking.

If the noodles are not done can add extra broth or water and then cook it longer.

Garnish it with the cilantro.

Nutritional Information:

Calories: 302

Total Fat: 19g

Saturated Fat: 7g

Carbohydrates: 19g

Protein: 14g

Crock Pot Minestrone Soup

Ingredients:

1 (15 oz) Can of White Beans – Drained, Rinsed

32 oz Container of Reduced Sodium Chicken Broth

2 tsp. of Olive Oil

1/2 Cups of Onion - Chopped

8 Ounces of Carrots - Diced

1/2 Cups of Celery - Diced

2 Cloves of Garlic - Minced

1 (28 oz) Can of Tomatoes - Diced

Parmesan Cheese

1 Rosemary Sprig

2 Bay Leaves

2 Tablespoons of Chopped Basil

1/4 Cups of Chopped Italian Parsley

1/2 tsp. of Salt and Black Pepper

1 Medium Zucchini - Diced

2 Cups of Chopped Spinach

2 Cups of Cooked Ditalini

Instructions:

Puree the beans with 8 ounces of broth in your blender. Heat the oil in a large skillet on medium-high heat. Add in the carrots, celery, the onion, your garlic and then saute it until it's tender, around 15 minutes.

Transfer it to the crock-pot with the remaining broth, the tomatoes, beans, parmesan cheese, salt, and the pepper. Add in the rosemary, the basil, and the parsley. Cover it and cook it on low for 6 - 8 hours.

Forty minutes prior to the soup being done, add the zucchini and the spinach. Cover it and cook it for 30 more minutes. Remove the bay leaves, rosemary sprig and then season it to taste with the salt and pepper. Ladle about 1-1/4 cups of soup into 8 bowls with some of the pasta. Top it with extra parmesan cheese.

Nutritional Information:

Calories: 190

Total Fat: 3g

Saturated Fat: 2g

Carbohydrates: 32g

Protein: 9g

Lentil Cauliflower Stew

Ingredients:

16 Ounces of Dried Lentils

1 Tablespoon of Olive Oil

1 Large Onion - Chopped

2 Cloves of Garlic - Chopped

1 lb. of Cauliflower - Chopped

2 Leeks - Halved, Washed, Chopped

2 Large Carrots – Peeled, Chopped

3 Celery Stalks - Chopped

2 Bay Leaves

1 Tablespoon of Thyme - Chopped

2 tsp. of Salt

1 tsp. of Cumin

1/2 tsp. of Cayenne

1/4 tsp. of Pepper

8 Cups of Low Sodium Vegetable Broth

1 Large Can (32 oz) of Diced Tomatoes with the Juice

2 Cups of Chopped Kale or Swiss Chard

Instructions:

Sort through the lentils, discarding the stones or debris.

Rinse your lentils in a strainer.

Heat the oil in a pan on medium heat. Sauté your onions for approximately 4 minutes. Add in the chopped garlic and the sauté for an additional minute.

Pour in the softened onions and the garlic into your slow cooker and then add in the remaining ingredients.

Cover your slow cooker and then turn the heat to high. Set your timer to 6 hours on the high setting, or for 8 hours on the low setting, until your lentils are soft.

Serve it hot with your toppings.

Nutritional Information:

Calories: 238

Total Fat: 9g

Saturated Fat: 1g

Carbohydrates: 35g

Protein: 9g

Crock Pot Lasagna

Ingredients:

1 lb of Lean Ground Beef

1 Onion - Chopped

2 Cloves of Garlic - Smashed

1 (28 ounce) Can of Tomato Sauce

1 (6 ounce) Can of Tomato Paste

1 1/2 Teaspoons of Salt

1 Teaspoon of Oregano - Dried

12 Ounces of Cottage Cheese

1/2 Cups of Grated Parmesan Cheese

12 Ounces of Lasagna Noodles - Uncooked

16 Ounces of Shredded Mozzarella Cheese

Instructions:

Brown the ground beef, onion, and the garlic a pan.

Add in the tomato sauce, the tomato paste, salt, and the oregano.

Cook it long enough warm it.

Spoon a layer of the meat sauce on the bottom of your slow cooker.

Add a double layer of the lasagna noodles uncooked (break it to fit) and then top it with cheese.

Repeat it with sauce, noodles and the cheeses until it is all used up.

Cover it and cook it on the low setting for 4 - 5 hours.

Nutritional Information:

Calories: 248

Total Fat: 10g

Saturated Fat: 3g

Carbohydrates: 22g

Protein: 18g

Slow Cooked Spinach Manicotti

Ingredients:

1 (15 oz) Ricotta Cheese

1 (10 oz) Package of Frozen Spinach - Thawed, Drained, Squeezed

1 Egg - Beaten

1/2 Cup of Grated Parmesan Cheese - Divided

1/2 Cup of Mozzarella Cheese - Shredded

1/2 tsp. of Salt

2 (14 1/2 oz) Cans of Stewed Tomatoes

1 (24 oz) Jar of Roasted Garlic and Herb Pasta Sauce - Divided

1 (8 oz) Package of Uncooked Manicotti Shells

Instructions:

Stir together the ricotta, spinach, the beaten egg, 1/4 cups of parmesan, the mozzarella and salt.

In the bottom of the slow cooker, combine 1 can of stewed tomatoes and 8 ounces of the pasta sauce.

Stuff the shells with the spinach mix, then put the stuffed shells in your cooker.

Top the shells with the second can of tomatoes, arrange the remaining stuffed shells on the tomatoes and pour the rest of the sauce over the manicotti; top it with 1/2 cups of the parmesan, cover it and cook it for 3-4 hrs.

Nutritional Information:

Calories: 389

Total Fat: 9g

Saturated Fat: 2g

Carbohydrates: 50g

Protein: 25g

Slow Cooked Mac and Cheese

Ingredients:

1-1/2 Cups of Milk

1 (12 oz.) Can of Evaporated Milk

1/4 Cups of Butter – Melted, Cooled

3 Eggs

1/2 tsp. of Salt

3 Cups of Shredded Italian Blend Cheese

1/2 Pound of Elbow Macaroni

Pepper

1/2 Cups of Parmesan Cheese

Instructions:

Grease the inside of the slow cooker with some cooking spray.

Combine the milk, the evaporated milk, butter, the eggs, and the salt in your slow cooker and whisk it until it is smooth.

Add in the Italian cheese and then the macaroni. Sprinkle it with pepper. Stir it gently to coat it evenly.

Sprinkle it with the Parmesan cheese.

Cover it and cook it on high for at least 30 minutes.

After the 30 minutes, reduce the temperature to the low setting and then cook it for 1 1/2-2 hours.

Serve it while it is hot.

Nutritional Information:

Calories: 329

Total Fat: 18g

Saturated Fat: 3g

Carbohydrates: 30g

Protein: 13g

/egetable and Pasta Soup

Ingredients:

1 - 10 Ounce Package of Whole Kernel Corn - Frozen

8 Ounces of Onion - Chopped

8 Ounces of Carrots – Chopped Fine

8 Ounces of Zucchini - Chopped

2 Cloves of Garlic - Minced

6 Cups of Vegetable Broth

1 (6 ounce) Can of Tomato Paste with Basil, Garlic, and Oregano

½ Teaspoon of Salt

½ Teaspoon of Basil - Crushed

1 (9 ounce) Package of Italian Green Beans - Chopped

8 Ounces of Tiny Shell Macaroni

2 Tablespoons of Parsley

2 Teaspoons of Shredded Parmesan Cheese

Instructions:

In your 3 1/2- to 5-quart slow cooker; combine the corn, onions, the carrots, zucchini, and the garlic. Stir in the broth, tomato paste, the salt, and basil.

Cover it and cook it on the low setting for 7 - 8 hours or on the high setting for 3 1/2 - 4 hours.

If you are using the low setting, turn it to the high setting. Stir in the frozen green beans and the macaroni. Cover it and cook it for 45 minutes longer. Before serving it, stir in the parsley. Sprinkle each serving with some cheese.

Nutritional Information:

Calories: 172

Total Fat: 1g

Saturated Fat: 1g

Carbohydrates: 36g

Protein: 6g

Pesto Chicken Sandwiches

Ingredients:

1 Teaspoon of Italian Seasoning

¼ Teaspoon of Salt

¼ Teaspoon of Black Pepper

1 Pound of Chicken Breast - Halved

1 Large Onion - Thinly sliced

8 Ounces of Mushrooms - Sliced

2 Cloves of Garlic - Minced

1 - 14 1/2 Ounce Can of Diced Tomatoes - Undrained

2 Tablespoons of red wine vinegar

1 Medium Zucchini – Halved, Lengthwise, Sliced 1/4 inch thick

1 Large Red, Yellow, and Green Sweet Pepper - Cut to Strips

1/3 Cups of Mayonnaise

2 Tablespoons of Pesto

1 - 12 inch Loaf of Ciabatta Bread - Cut in Half Horizontally

Basil Leave

Instructions:

In a small mixing bowl combine the Italian seasoning, salt, and the pepper. Sprinkle the mixture over the sides of chicken; rub it into the chicken using your fingers. Put the chicken in your 3-1/2- or 4-quart slow cooker.

Add the onion, mushrooms, and the garlic. In a mixing bowl combine the tomatoes and then vinegar; pour it over your chicken mixture in your cooker.

Cover it and cook it on the low setting for 4 - 5 hours or on the high setting for 2 - 2-1/2 hours. If you are using the low setting, turn it to the high setting. Stir in the zucchini and the sweet pepper. Cover it and cook it on the high setting for 30 minutes longer.

Meanwhile, in a small mixing bowl combine the mayonnaise and the pesto. Spread the pesto mix evenly on the cut sides of your bread.

Transfer the chicken to your cutting board. Using a slotted spoon, spoon the vegetable mixture onto the bread bottom. Discard the cooking juices. Thinly slice the chicken. Arrange your chicken slices on the vegetables. Add the basil and bread top. Cut the loaf into 6 - 8 serving sized portions.

Nutritional Information:

Calories: 235

Total Fat: 3g

Saturated Fat: 1g

Carbohydrates: 2g

Protein: 30g

Mushroom Risotto with Peas

Ingredients:

3 Tablespoons of Butter

3 Cups of Sliced Mushrooms

1/3 Cups of Sliced Shallots

2 Cloves of Garlic - Minced

1 ¾ Cups of Arborio Rice - Uncooked

4 Cups of Chicken Broth

¾ Cup of Dry White Wine

½ Teaspoon of Black Pepper

2/3 Cups of Peas – Frozen, Thawed

Asiago Cheese Shards

Fresh Parsley Leaves

Instructions:

In a large pan heat the butter on medium heat until it is melted. Add the mushrooms, shallots, and the garlic; cook it for 5 - 7 minutes, stirring sporadically. Stir in the rice; cook it and stir it for 1 minute longer. Transfer the rice mix to your 3 1/2- or 4-quart slow cooker. Stir in the broth, wine, and the pepper.

Cover it and cook it on the low setting approximately 2 3/4 hours or on the high setting for about 1 1/4 hours. If possible, remove the crockery liner from your cooker. Stir in the peas. If you want, top it with cheese and parsley.

Nutritional Information:

Calories: 223

Total Fat: 5g

Saturated Fat: 2g

Carbohydrates: 37g

Protein: 5g

Chicken Osso Buco

Ingredients:

12 Medium Chicken Drumsticks

2 Tablespoons of Flour

½ Teaspoon of Salt

¼ Teaspoon of Pepper

2 Tablespoons of Olive Oil

8 Ounces of Carrot - Chopped

8 ounces of Onion - Chopped

8 Ounces of Celery - Chopped

6 Cloves of Garlic - Minced

2 Tablespoons of Quick-Cooking Tapioca

1 - 8 Ounce Can of Tomato Sauce

½ Cup of Dry White Wine

¼ Cup of Chicken Broth

1 Teaspoon of Shredded Lemon Peel

1 Tablespoon of Lemon Juice

1 Teaspoon of Thyme - Crushed

3 Cups of Penne Pasta

Fresh Parsley

Instructions:

Remove the skin from the chicken. Put the flour, salt, and the pepper in a re-sealable plastic bag. Add the chicken, a few pieces at time, shake it to coat it. In a 10-inch pan, brown the chicken, half at a time in the hot oil on medium heat approximately 10 minutes, turning once. Put it aside.

In your 4- to 5-quart slow cooker, combine the carrot, onion, the celery, and the garlic. Sprinkle it with tapioca. Put the chicken on the top of the vegetables. In a medium mixing bowl, stir together the tomato sauce, the wine, broth, lemon peel, the lemon juice, and the thyme; pour it over your chicken in the cooker.

Cover it and cook it on the low setting for 5 - 6 hours or on the high setting for 2-1/2 to 3 hours.

Prepare the penne according to the package directions. Drain it well. Spoon the chicken and the sauce on the pasta. If you want, garnish it with the parsley.

Nutritional Information:

Calories: 407

Total Fat: 2g

Saturated Fat: 1g

Carbohydrates: 42g

Protein: 33g

Warm Eggplant and Kale Panzanella

Ingredients:

4 Cups of Eggplant - Chopped

1 - (14 ½) Ounce Can of Diced Fire-Roasted Tomatoes with Garlic - undrained

3/4 Cups of Yellow Sweet Pepper – Chopped

1 Medium Red Onion - Cut into Thin Wedges

4 Cups of Kale Leaves – Fresh, Chopped

3 Tablespoons of Red Wine Vinegar

2 Tablespoons of Olive Oil

1 Teaspoon of Dijon-Style Mustard

1/2 Teaspoons of Pepper

1 Clove of Garlic - Minced

½ Cup of Basil – Sprigs, Chopped

4 Cups of Cubed Whole Wheat French Bread - Toasted

½ Cup of Parmesan Cheese

Instructions:

In your 3 1/2- or 4-quart slow cooker combine the eggplant, tomatoes, the sweet peppers, and the red onion. Cover it and cook it on the low setting for 4 hours.

If you are using the low setting, turn it to the high setting. Stir in the kale. Cover it and cook it for 15 minutes longer.

Meanwhile, as far as the dressing, in your small mixing bowl whisk together the vinegar, oil, the mustard, pepper, and the garlic.

Using a slotted spoon, transfer the vegetable mix to a large mixing bowl. Add in the dressing and the basil; toss it gently to coat it well. Add in the toasted bread; toss it gently to combine it well.

Transfer the mix to a serving platter. Sprinkle it with cheese. Serve immediately.

Nutritional Information:

Calories: 243

Total Fat: 9g

Saturated Fat: 2g

Carbohydrates: 34g

Protein: 9g

Slow Cooker Ribollita

Ingredients:

1 Pound of Cannellini Beans – Rinsed, Drained

1 Head of Garlic - Halved Horizontally

1 Sprigs of Sage

4 Cups of Reduced-Sodium Chicken Broth

1 (28 ounce) Can of Whole Peeled Tomatoes - Puree

6 Tablespoons of Olive Oil

Salt

Pepper

2/3 Cups of Pancetta - Chopped

8 Ounces of Onion - Chopped

8 Ounces of Carrots - Chopped

8 Ounces of Celery - Chopped

2 Teaspoons of Thyme

2 Cloves of Garlic - Minced

4 Cups of Kale - Chopped

8 Ounces of Parsley

8 Slices of Italian Bread

1 Clove of Garlic

½ Cup of Grated Parmesan Cheese

Olive oil

Instructions:

Place the beans in a large Dutch oven; add enough water in order to cover them. Bring it to boil; boil it gently for 10 minutes. Cover it and then let stand for 1 hour.

Drain and rinse the beans. Set it aside. Cut it in an 8-inch square from a double thickness of cheesecloth. Place the halved garlic heads and sage in the center of the cheesecloth square. Bring up the corners; tie it closed with a 100% cotton kitchen string. In your 5-6-quart slow cooker combine the beans, garlic sage packet, the broth, tomatoes, 2 tablespoons of olive oil, 1/2 teaspoons of salt, and 1/4 teaspoon of the pepper. Cover it and cook it on the low setting for 10 - 12 hours or on the high setting for 5 - 6 hours or until beans are soft.

Discard the garlic-sage packet. Use a potato masher to mash some of your beans.

In a large pan heat 2 tablespoons of olive oil on medium heat. Add the pancetta; cook it and stir it for 3 - 5 minutes. Add the onion, carrots, the celery, and 1/2 teaspoons of salt. Cook it and stir it for 5 minutes. Stir in the thyme and minced garlic; cook it 30 seconds longer.

If you are using the low setting, turn the cooker to the high setting. Stir in the vegetable mix into the slow cooker. Cover it and cook it for about 1 hour more. Stir in the kale and the parsley.

Meanwhile, preheat your oven to 350 degrees Fahrenheit. Arrange the bread slices on a baking sheet; brush both sides of the slices lightly with oil. Bake it approximately 10 minutes; turn it once halfway through the time. Cool the bread slightly; rub the garlic clove over one side of the toast. Put one toast in each bowl. Ladle the hot soup on the toast. Sprinkle the individual servings with Parmesan cheese.

Nutritional Information:

Calories: 452 Total Fat: 13g Saturated Fat: 3g Carbohydrates: 63g Protein: 22g

Italian Wedding Soup

Ingredients:

2 Eggs - Beaten

8 Ounces of Onion - Chopped

1/3 Cups of Bread Crumbs

2 Tablespoons of Parmesan Cheese

2 Tablespoons of Fresh Parsley

1 Teaspoon of Salt

¾ Teaspoon of Pepper

1 ½ Pound of Lean Ground Beef

1 Tablespoon of Vegetable Oil

8 Cups of Reduced-Sodium Chicken Broth

3 Large Carrots - Chopped

2 Tablespoons of Oregano

1 Small Head Escarole – Trimmed, Cut into 1/2-inch Strips

8 Ounces of Acini Di Pepe Pasta

 Fresh Oregano Sprigs

Instructions:

In a large mixing bowl, combine the eggs, onion, the breadcrumbs, cheese, the parsley, 1/2 teaspoons of the salt, and 1/2 teaspoons of pepper. Add the ground beef; mix it well. Shape the mixture into forty 1-1/4-inch meatballs. In a large pan, heat 1 tablespoon of oil; brown the meatballs, half at one time. Drain it on paper towels.

In your 5- 6-quart slow cooker, combine the broth, carrots, the oregano, the remaining 1/2 teaspoons of salt, and remaining 1/4 teaspoon pepper. Gently add in the meatballs.

Cover it and cook it on the low setting for 6 hours or on the high setting for 3 hours, stirring in the oregano, the pasta, and escarole during the last 20 minutes of the cooking time. Ladle it into bowls. If you want, garnish it with the oregano sprigs. The soup will thicken after standing

Nutritional Information:

Calories: 330

Total Fat: 10g

Saturated Fat: 3g Carbohydrates: 31g Protein: 28g

Penne with Tomato-Eggplant Sauce

Instructions:

1 Medium Eggplant

1 (28 ounce) Can Italian-Style Whole Peeled Tomatoes - Undrained, Diced

1 (6 ounce) Can Tomato Paste

1 (4 ounce can) Mushrooms - drained

½ Cup of Onion - CHOPPED

¼ Cup of Dry Red Wine

¼ Cup of Water

1 ½ Teaspoon of Oregano - Crushed

2 Cloves of Garlic - Minced

¼ Teaspoon of Salt

1/8 Teaspoon of Pepper

¼ Cup of Pitted Kalamata Olives Or Ripe Olives, Sliced

2 Tablespoons of Parsley

4 Cups of Whole Grain Penne Pasta - Cooked

¼ Cup of Parmesan Cheese

Instructions:

If you want, peel the eggplant. Cut the eggplant into 1-inch pieces. In your 3-1/2- to 5 1/2-quart slow cooker combine the eggplant, tomato paste, tomatoes, mushrooms, the onions, wine, water, the oregano, garlic, some salt, and pepper.

Cover it and cook it on the low setting for 7 - 8 hours or on the high setting for 3-1/2 - 4 hours.

Stir in the olives and the parsley. Serve it on the hot cooked pasta. If your want, sprinkle with it with cheese.

Nutritional Information:

Calories: 222

Total Fat: 2g

Saturated Fat: 2g

Carbohydrates: 44g

Protein: 8g

Beef and Carrot Ragu

Ingredients:

1 Pound of Beef Short Ribs - Boneless

Salt and Pepper

10 Cloves of Garlic

8 Ounces pkg. of Peeled Baby Carrots - Chopped

1 Pound of Roma Tomatoes - chopped

6 Ounce Can of Tomato Paste with Basil, Garlic, and Oregano

1/2 Cups of Water

Basil Leaves

Instructions:

Trim the excess fat off rib meat. Cut the beef into chunks, and then sprinkle it lightly with dame salt and pepper. Place the beef in your 3 1/2- or 4-quart slow cooker.

Smash the garlic cloves with a flat side of a chef's knife. Separate it and discard the garlic skins. Place the smashed garlic on the beef. Add in the carrots and the tomatoes to slow cooker.

In a medium-mixing bowl, whisk together the tomato paste and the water. Pour it over the meat and the vegetables. Cover it and cook it on the high setting for 3 - 4 hours or on the low setting for 6 - 8 hours.

Stir it well before serving it. Top it with the basil.

Nutritional Information:

Calories: 509

Total Fat: 42g

Saturated Fat: 18g

Carbohydrates: 15g

Protein: 19g

Italian Pork and Sweet Potatoes

Ingredients:

1 Teaspoon of Fennel Seeds - Crushed

½ teaspoon of Garlic Powder

½ Teaspoon of Oregano - Crushed

½ Teaspoon of Paprika

¼ Teaspoon of Salt

¼ Teaspoon of Pepper

1 (1 ½) Pound of Pork Shoulder Roast - Boneless

1 Pound of Sweet Potatoes – Peeled, Cut into 1-inch Pieces

8 Ounces of Reduced-Sodium Chicken Broth

Parsley Sprigs

Instructions:

In a small mixing bowl, combine the fennel seeds, garlic powder, the oregano, paprika, some salt, and some pepper. Trim the fat from the meat. Sprinkle the fennel seed mix evenly on the meat; rub it in with your fingers. If it is necessary, cut the meat to fit into your 3 1/2- or 4-quart slow cooker.

Place the sweet potatoes in your cooker. Add in the meat. Pour the broth on the meat mixture in your cooker.

Cover it and cook it on the low setting for 8 - 10 hours or on the high setting for 4 - 5 hours.

Remove meat from cooker, reserving cooking juices. Slice or **shred meat**. Serve meat with sweet potatoes. If desired, garnish with sprigs of parsley.

Nutritional Information:

Calories: 341

Total Fat: 10g

Saturated Fat: 1g

Carbohydrates: 24g

Protein: 36g

Spaghetti with Sauce Italiano

Ingredients:

1 Pound of Italian Sausage

8 Ounces of Onion - Chopped

2 Cloves of Garlic - Minced

2 (14 1/2 ounce) Cans of Diced Tomatoes - Undrained

2 (4 ounce) Cans of Mushroom Stems and Pieces - Drained

1 (6 ounce) Can of Tomato Paste

1 Bay Leaf

1 Tablespoon of Oregano

½ Teaspoon of Salt

¼ Teaspoon of Pepper

8 Ounces of Green Sweet Pepper - Chopped

12 Ounces of Dried Spaghetti

Shredded Parmesan Cheese

Instructions:

In a large pan, cook the meat, onion, and the garlic on medium heat until the meat is brown and the onion is soft. Drain off the fat.

Meanwhile, in your 3 1/2- or 4-quart slow cooker, combine he undrained tomatoes, mushrooms, tomato paste, the bay leaf, oregano, some salt, and the black pepper. Stir in the meat mix.

Cover it and cook it on the low setting for 8 - 10 hours or on the high setting for 4 - 5 hours. Discard the bay leaf. Turn off the cooker. Add in the sweet pepper; cover it and allow it to stand for 5 minutes.

Meanwhile, cook the pasta, lightly salt the water; drain it when it's done. Spoon the meat mixture on the pasta. Sprinkle it with cheese.

Nutritional Information:

Calories: 621

Total Fat: 30g

Saturated Fat: 15g

Carbohydrates: 62g

Protein: 28g

Saucy Ravioli with Meatballs

Ingredients:

Non-Stick Cooking Spray

2 (26 ounce) Jars Spaghetti Sauce with Mushrooms

2 (24 ounce) Packages Ravioli - Frozen

1 (12 ounce) Package Italian Meatballs – Frozen, Thawed

2 Cups of Mozzarella Cheese

½ Cup of Parmesan Cheese

Instructions:

Lightly coat your 5 1/2- or 6-quart slow cooker with the cooking spray. Add in 8 ounces of the spaghetti sauce. Add in the ravioli from one package and the meatballs. Sprinkle it with 8 ounces of mozzarella cheese. Top it with the remaining spaghetti sauce from first jar. Add in the ravioli from remaining package and the remaining 8 ounces of mozzarella cheese. Pour the spaghetti sauce from second jar on the mixture in your cooker.

Cover it; cook it on the low setting for 4 1/2 - 5 hours or on the high setting for 2 1/2 - 3 hours. Turn off your cooker. Sprinkle the ravioli mixture with the Parmesan cheese. Cover it; and let it stand for 15 minutes prior to serving it.

Nutritional Information:

Calories: 510

Total Fat: 18g

Saturated Fat: 2g

Carbohydrates: 67g

Protein: 26g

Caponata Sicilianata

Ingredients:

1 Pound of Roma Tomatoes - Chopped

12 Ounces of Eggplant - Cut into 1/2-inch Pieces

12 Ounces of Zucchini - Cut into 1/2-inch Pieces

1 ½ Cup of Celery - Sliced

¾ Cup of Onion - Chopped

½ Cup of Parsley

¼ Cup of Raisins

¼ Cup of Tomato Paste

2 Tablespoons of Red Wine Vinegar

1 Tablespoon of Brown Sugar

1 Teaspoon of Salt

¼ Teaspoon of Pepper

3 Tablespoon of Pitted Ripe Olives - Chopped

2 Tablespoons of Drained Capers

Instructions:

r 3 1/2- or 4-quart slow cooker, combine the tomatoes, eggplant, the zucchini, celery, onion, the parsley, raisins, the tomato paste, vinegar, the brown sugar, the salt, and the pepper.

Cover it and cook it on the low setting for 5 1/2 hours or on the high setting for 3 1/2 hours. If you want, stir in the olives and the capers. Serve it warm, cold, or even at room temperature.

Nutritional Information:

Calories: 276

Total Fat: 3g

Saturated Fat: 1g

Carbohydrates: 14g

Protein: 25g

.

Italian Braised Chicken with Fennel and Cannellini

Ingredients:

2 Pound of Chicken Drumsticks - Skin Removed

¾ Teaspoon of Salt

¼ Teaspoon of Pepper

1 (15 ounce) Can of Cannellini Beans – Rinsed, Drained

1 Bulb Fennel – Cored, Cut into Wedges

1 medium yellow sweet pepper, seeded and cut into 1-inch pieces

1 Medium Onion - Cut into Wedges

3 Cloves of Garlic - Minced

1 Teaspoon of Rosemary

1 Teaspoon of Oregano

¼ Teaspoon of Red Pepper - Crushed

1 (14 ½) Ounce Can of Diced Tomatoes

½ Cup of Dry White Wine

¼ Cup of Tomato Paste

¼ Cup of Parmesan Cheese

1 Tablespoon of Parsley

Instructions:

Sprinkle the chicken pieces with 1/4 teaspoon of salt and the pepper. Place the chicken in your 3 1/2- to 4-quart slow cooker. Top it with cannellini beans, fennel, the sweet pepper, onion, the garlic, rosemary, oregano, and the crushed red pepper. In a medium mixing bowl, combine tomatoes, the white wine, tomato paste, and the remaining 1/2 teaspoons of salt; pour it on the mixture in your cooker.

Cover it; cook it on the low setting for 5 - 6 hours or on the high setting for 2 1/2 - 3 hours.

Sprinkle each of the servings with Parmesan cheese and the parsley.

Nutritional Information:

Calories: 225

Total Fat: 4g

Saturated Fat: 1g

Carbohydrates: 23g

Protein: 25g

Char Siu Pork Roast

Ingredients:

1/4 cups of lower-sodium soy sauce

1/4 cups of hoisin sauce

3 tablespoon of ketchup

3 tablespoon of honey

2 teaspoons of minced garlic

2 teaspoons of grated peeled fresh ginger

1 teaspoon of dark sesame oil

1/2 teaspoons of five-spice powder

1 (2-pound of) boneless pork shoulder (Boston butt), trimmed

1/2 cups of fat-free, lower-sodium chicken broth

Instructions:

Combine first 8 ingredients in a small bowl, stirring well with a whisk. Place in a large zip-top plastic bag. Add pork to bag; seal. Marinate in refrigerator at least 2 hours, turning occasionally.

Place pork and marinade in an electric slow cooker. Cover and cook on low for 8 hours.

Remove pork from slow cooker using a slotted spoon; place on a cutting board or work surface. Cover with aluminum foil; keep warm.

Add broth to sauce in slow cooker. Cover and cook on low for 30 minutes or until sauce thickens. Shred pork with 2 forks; serve with sauce.

Nutritional Information:

Calories: 227

Total Fat: 9g

Saturated Fat: 2g

Carbohydrates: 21g

Protein: 2g

Mediterranean Roast Turkey

Ingredients:

2 Cups of Onion - Chopped

1/2 Cups of Pitted Kalamata Olives

1/2 Cups of Sun-Dried Tomato Halves

2 Tablespoons of Lemon Juice

1 1/2 Teaspoons of Garlic - Minced

1 Teaspoon of Greek Seasoning Mix

1/2 Teaspoons of Salt

1/4 Teaspoon of Pepper

1 (4-pound of) Turkey Breast – Boneless, Trimmed

1/2 Cups of Chicken Broth - Divided

3 Tablespoon of Flour

Thyme Sprigs

Instructions:

Combine the first 9 ingredients in your slow cooker. Add in 1/4 cups of chicken broth. Cover it and cook it on the low setting for 7 hours.

Combine the remaining 1/4 cups of broth and the flour in a small mixing bowl; stir it with a whisk until it is smooth. Add in the broth mixture to your slow cooker. Cover it and cook on low for 30 minutes. Cut turkey into slices.

Nutritional Information:

Calories: 314

Total Fat: 5g

Saturated Fat: 1g

Carbohydrates: 7g

Protein: 26g

Vegetable and Chickpea Curry

Ingredients:

1 Tablespoon of Olive Oil

1 1/2 Cups of Onion - Chopped

8 Ounces of Carrot - Sliced

1 Tablespoon of Curry Powder

1 Teaspoon of Brown Sugar

1 Teaspoon of Fresh Ginger – Grated, Peeled

2 Cloves of Garlic – Minced

1 Serrano Chile – Seeded, Minced

3 Cups of Chickpeas - Cooked

1 1/2 Cups of Baking Potato – Peeled, Cubed

8 Ounces of Green Bell Pepper - Diced

8 Ounces of Green Beans - Cut

1/2 Teaspoons of Salt

1/4 Teaspoon of Pepper

1/8 Teaspoon of Red Pepper

1 (141/2-ounce) Can of Diced Tomatoes - Undrained

1 (14-ounce) Can of Vegetable Broth

3 Cups of Spinach - Fresh

8 Ounces of Light Coconut Milk

6 Lemon Wedges

Instructions:

Heat the oil in a large pan over medium heat. Add the onion and the carrots; cover it and cook it for 5 minutes. Add the curry powder, sugar, the ginger, garlic, and the chile; cook it for 1 minute, stirring it constantly.

Place the onion mixture in your 5-quart electric slow cooker. Stir in the chickpeas and then 8 ingredients. Cover it and cook it on the high setting for 6 hours or until the vegetables are soft. Add in the spinach and the coconut milk; stir it until the spinach wilts. Serve it with lemon wedges.

Nutritional Information:

Calories: 276

Total Fat: 7g

Saturated Fat: 1g

Carbohydrates: 44g

Protein: 2g

Provençal Beef Daube

Ingredients:

2 Pound of Chuck Roast – Trimmed, Cut into Chunks

1 Tablespoon of Extra-Virgin Olive Oil

6 Cloves of Garlic - Minced

1/2 Cups of Boiling Water

1/2 Ounce of Porcini Mushrooms

3/4 Teaspoon of Salt - Divided

Cooking Spray

1/2 Cups of Red Wine

1/4 Cups of Beef Broth

1/3 Cups of Pitted Niçoise Olives

1/2 Teaspoons of Pepper

2 Large Carrots – Peeled, Thinly Sliced

1 Large Onion – Peeled, Chopped

1 Celery Stalk - Sliced

1 (15-ounce) Can of Whole Tomatoes – Drained, Crushed

1 Teaspoon of Whole Black Peppercorns

3 Parsley Sprigs

3 Thyme Sprigs

1 Bay Leaf

1 (1-inch) Strip Orange Rind

1 Tablespoon of Water

1 Teaspoon of Cornstarch

1 1/2 Tablespoon of Parsley Leaves - Chopped

1 1/2 Teaspoons of Thyme - Chopped

Instructions:

1. Combine the first 3 ingredients in a large zip-top bag. Seal it and marinate it at room temperature for 30 minutes, turning the bag occasionally.

2. Combine 1/2 cup of the boiling water and the mushrooms; cover it and let it stand for 30 minutes. Drain it through a strainer on top of a bowl, reserve the mushrooms and 1/4 cups of the soaking liquid. Chop the mushrooms.

3. Heat a large pan on medium-high heat. Sprinkle the beef mix with 1/4 teaspoon of salt. Coat the pan with spray. Add in half of the beef mixture to the pan; sauté it for 5 minutes, turn it to brown on all the sides. Place the browned beef mixture in your 6-quart slow cooker. Repeat the procedure with the spray and left over beef mixture. Add it the wine and the broth to a pan; bring to a boil, scrap the pan to loosen the browned bits. Pour in the wine mixture into your slow cooker. Add in the mushrooms, reserved 1/4 cups of the soaking liquid, the remaining 1/2 teaspoons of salt, olives, and the next 5 ingredients. Place the peppercorns, parsley sprigs, the thyme sprigs, the bay leaf, and orange rind on double layer cheesecloth. Gather the edges of cheesecloth together; then secure it with twine. Add the cheesecloth bundle to your slow cooker. Cover it and cook it on the low setting for 6 hours or until the beef and the vegetables are soft. Discard the cheesecloth.

4. Combine 1 tablespoon of water and the cornstarch in a small mixing bowl, stirring it until it is smooth. Add in the cornstarch mixture to your slow cooker; cook it for 20 minutes or until it is slightly thick, stir it occasionally. Sprinkle it with chopped parsley and some chopped thyme.

Nutritional Information:

Calories: 360

Total Fat: 8g

Saturated Fat: 2g

Carbohydrates: 8g

Protein: 30g

Smoky Slow Cooker Chili

Ingredients:

1 Pound of Ground Pork

1 Pound of Pork Shoulder – Boneless, Cut into 1/2-inch Pieces

3 Cups of Onion - Chopped

1 3/4 Cups of Green Bell Pepper - Chopped

3 Cloves of Garlic - Minced

3 Tablespoon of Tomato Paste

3 Tablespoon of Chili Powder

1 Tablespoon of Cumin

2 Teaspoons of Oregano

3/4 Teaspoon of Pepper

6 Tomatillos - Quartered

2 Bay Leaves

2 (14 1/2-ounce) Cans of Plum Tomatoes – Undrained, Chopped

1 (15-ounce) Can of Pinto Beans - Drained

1 (7 3/4-ounce) Can of Mexican Hot-Style Tomato Sauce

1 Smoked Ham Hock

1 1/2 Tablespoon of Sugar

1/2 Cups of Cilantro – Chopped Fine

1/2 Cups of Green Onions - Chopped

2 Ounces of Crumbled Low Fat Queso Fresco

8 Lime Wedges

Instructions:

Heat a large pan on medium-high heat. Coat the pan with spray. Add in the ground pork to the pan; cook it for 5 minutes, make sure you stir it to slightly crumble. Drain it well. Transfer the pork to a slow cooker.

Recoat the pan with spray. Add the pork shoulder; cook it for 5 minutes or until it lightly browned, turn it occasionally. Transfer the pork to your slow cooker.

Recoat the pan with spray. Add in the onion and the bell pepper; sauté it for 8 minutes, stirring it frequently. Add in the garlic; sauté it for 1 minute. Add in the tomato paste; cook it for 1 minute, stirring it constantly. Transfer the onion mixture to your slow cooker. Add in the chili powder, and the next 9 ingredients to slow cooker. Cover it and cook it on the high setting for 5 hours. Remove the bay leaves and the ham hock; discard it. Stir in the sugar. Ladle about 1 1/3 cups of the chili into each of the 8 bowls; top each serving with 1 tablespoon of the cilantro, 1 tablespoon of green onions, and cheese. Serve each of the servings with 1 lime wedge.

Nutritional Information:

Calories: 357

Total Fat: 14g

Saturated Fat: 2g

Carbohydrates: 27g

Protein: 27g

Provençale Chicken

Makes 4 servings

Ingredients:

4 (6-ounce) Chicken Breast - Halves, Skinned

2 Teaspoons of Basil

1/8 Teaspoon of Salt

1/8 Teaspoon of Pepper

8 Ounces of Yellow Bell Pepper - Chopped

1 (151/2-ounce) Can of Cannellini Beans – Rinsed, Drained

1 (141/2-ounce) Can of Diced Tomatoes with Basil, Garlic, and Oregano - Undrained

Basil Sprigs

Instructions:

Place your chicken in a slow cooker; sprinkle it with basil, salt, and the black pepper. Add the bell pepper, the beans, and the tomatoes. Cover it with lid; cook it on the low setting for 8 hours.

Nutritional Information:

Calories: 281

Total Fat: 2g

Saturated Fat: 1g

Carbohydrates: 18g

Protein: 44g

Pesto Lasagna with Spinach and Mushrooms

Ingredients:

4 cups of torn spinach

2 cups of sliced cremini mushrooms

1/2 cups of commercial pesto

3/4 cups of (3 ounces of) shredded part-skim mozzarella cheese

3/4 cups of (3 ounces of) shredded provolone cheese

1 (15-ounce) carton fat-free ricotta cheese

1 large egg, lightly beaten

3/4 cups of (3 ounces of) grated fresh Parmesan cheese, divided

1 (251/2-ounce) bottle fat-free tomato-basil pasta sauce

1 (8-ounce) can tomato sauce

Cooking spray

1 (8-ounce) package precooked lasagna noodles (12 noodles)

Instructions:

Arrange the spinach in a vegetable steamer; steam, covered, 3 minutes or until spinach wilts. Drain, squeeze dry, and coarsely chop. Combine spinach, mushrooms, and pesto in a medium bowl, stirring to combine; set aside.

Combine mozzarella, provolone, ricotta, and beaten egg in a medium bowl, stirring well to combine. Stir in 1/4 cups of Parmesan, and set aside. Combine the pasta sauce and the tomato sauce in a medium bowl.

Spread 8 ounces of of pasta sauce mixture in the bottom of a 6-quart oval electric slow cooker coated with cooking spray. Arrange 3 noodles over pasta sauce mixture; top with 8 ounces of of cheese mixture and 8 ounces of of spinach mixture. Repeat the layers, ending with spinach mixture. Arrange 3 noodles over spinach mixture; top with remaining 8 ounces of of cheese mixture and 8 ounces of of pasta sauce mixture. Place remaining 3 noodles over sauce mixture; spread remaining sauce mixture over noodles. Sprinkle with the remaining 1/2 cups of Parmesan. Cover with lid; cook on LOW 5 hours or until done.

Nutritional Information:

Calories: 398

Total Fat: 18g

Saturated Fat: 7g

Carbohydrates: 22g

Protein: 22g

Curried Beef Short Ribs

Ingredients:

2 Teaspoons of Canola Oil

2 Pounds of Beef Short Ribs - Trimmed

1/2 Teaspoons of Salt - Divided

1/4 Teaspoon of Pepper - Divided

1/3 Cups of Shallots - Minced

3 Tablespoon of Garlic - Minced

3 Tablespoon of Fresh Ginger – Minced, Peeled

1/4 Cups of Water

2 Tablespoons of Red Curry Paste

1/4 Cups of Light Coconut Milk

1 Tablespoon of Sugar

1 Tablespoon of Fish Sauce

1 Teaspoon of Grated Lime Rind

1 Tablespoon of Lime Juice

4 Cups of Jasmine Rice - Cooked

Instructions:

1. Heat the oil in a large nonstick pan on the medium-high heat. Sprinkle the ribs with 3/4 teaspoon of salt and 1/8 teaspoon of the pepper. Add half of the ribs to the pan; cook it for 2 minutes on each side. Place the ribs in a slow cooker. Repeat the procedure with the remaining ribs.

2. Add the shallots, garlic, and the ginger to the pan; sauté it for 2 minutes. Stir in 1/4 cups of the water and the curry paste; cook it for 1 minute. Stir in the coconut milk, sugar, and the fish sauce. Add the coconut milk mixture to your cooker. Cover it and cook it on the low setting for 6 hours.

3. Remove the ribs from your cooker; keep it warm. Strain the cooking liquid through your colander over a large bowl; discard the solids. Place a plastic bag inside a 2-cup of glass measuring cup. Pour the cooking liquid into the bag; let it stand for 10 minutes (fat will rise). Seal the bag; carefully snip off one corner of bag. Drain the drippings into a small mixing bowl, stop before the fat layer reaches the opening; discard the fat. Stir in the remaining 3/4 teaspoon of salt, the remaining 1/8 teaspoon of pepper, rind, and the juice. Shred the rib meat with two forks; discard the bones. Serve the sauce over the ribs and the rice.

Nutritional Information:

Calories: 446

Total Fat: 17g

Saturated Fat: 7g

Carbohydrates: 36g

Protein: 32g

Barley Stuffed Cabbage Rolls

Ingredients:

1 Large Head Green Cabbage - Cored

1 Tablespoon of Olive Oil

1 1/2 Cups of Onion - Chopped

3 Cups of Pearl Barley - Cooked

3 Ounces of Crumbled Feta Cheese

1/2 Cups of Currants - Dried

2 Tablespoons of Pine Nuts - Toasted

2 Tablespoons of Fresh Parsley - Chopped

1/4 Teaspoon of Salt - Divided

1/4 Teaspoon of Pepper - Divided

1/2 Cups of Apple Juice

1 Tablespoon of Cider Vinegar

1 (141/2-ounce) Can of Crushed Tomatoes - Undrained

Instructions: Steam the cabbage head for 8 minutes; cool it slightly. Remove 16 leaves from the cabbage head; discard the remaining cabbage. Cut off the raised portion of the center vein of each of the cabbage leaves; set the trimmed cabbage leaves to the side.

Heat the oil in a large nonstick pan on medium heat. Add the onion; cover it and cook it for 6 minutes or until soft. Remove it from the heat; stir in the barley and next the 4 ingredients. Stir in 1/4 teaspoon of salt and then 1/8 teaspoon of pepper.

Place the cabbage leaves on a flat surface; spoon approximately 1/3 cups of the barley mixture into the center of each cabbage leaf. Fold in the edges of leaves over the barley mixture; roll it up. Arrange the cabbage rolls in bottom of your 5-quart slow cooker.

Combine the remaining 1/4-teaspoon of the salt, the remaining 1/8-teaspoon of pepper, apple juice, the vinegar, and the tomatoes; pour it evenly over the cabbage rolls. Cover it and cook it on the high setting for 2 hours.

Nutritional Information:

Calories: 479

Total Fat: 13g

Saturated Fat: 5g

Carbohydrates: 83g

Protein: 14g

Spinach Artichoke Dip

Ingredients:

11 (6-inch) Pita Bread Rounds

1/3 Cups of Sun-Dried Tomatoes - Chopped

8 Ounces of of Boiling Water

1 (14-ounce) Can of Quartered Artichoke Hearts – Drained, Chopped

1 (10-ounce) Package of Spinach – Chopped, Frozen, Thawed, Drained

1 (8-ounce) Tub of Light Cream Cheese - Softened

1 (8-ounce) Carton of Low-Fat Sour Cream

3/4 Cups of Parmesan Cheese

3/4 Cups of Fat-Free Milk

1/2 Cups of Crumbled Feta Cheese

1/2 Cups of Onion - Diced

1/2 Cups of Mayonnaise

1 Tablespoon of Red Wine Vinegar

1/4 Teaspoon of Pepper

2 Cloves of Garlic - Crushed

Instructions:

Preheat your oven to 350° Fahrenheit.

Split each of the pita breads in half horizontally; cut each of the halves into 6 wedges. Put the pita wedges in a single layer on your baking sheet; bake it at 350° for 10 minutes.

Combine the tomatoes and the boiling water in a large bowl; let it stand for 1 hour.

Place the artichokes and the next 11 ingredients in your 3 1/2-quart slow cooker; stir it well. Cover it with a lid; cook it on the low setting for 1 hour. Drain the tomatoes; stir it into the dip. Cover it and cook it for 1 hour. Serve it warm with the toasted pita wedges.

Nutritional Information:

Calories: 166

Total Fat: 7g

Saturated Fat: 4g

Carbohydrates: 22g

Protein: 26g

Creole Red Beans and Rice

Ingredients:

3 Cups of Water

8 Ounces of Red Kidney Beans

8 Ounces of Onion - Chopped

8 Ounces of Green Bell Pepper - Chopped

3/4 Cups of Celery - Chopped

1 Teaspoon of Thyme

1 Teaspoon of Paprika

3/4 Teaspoon of Ground Red Pepper

1/2 Teaspoons of Pepper

1/2 (14-ounce) Package of Turkey, Pork, and Beef Smoked Sausage – Sliced Thin

1 Bay Leaf

5 Cloves of Garlic - Minced

1/2 Teaspoons of Salt

3 Cups of Basmati Rice - Cooked

1/4 Cups of Green Onions - Chopped

Instructions:

Combine the first 12 ingredients in your slow cooker.

Cover it with a lid; cook it on high heat at least for 5 hours.

Discard the bay leaf; stir in the salt. Serve over rice; sprinkle the servings evenly with the green onions.

Nutritional Information:

Calories: 413

Total Fat: 21g

Saturated Fat: 2g

Carbohydrates: 76g

Protein: 21g

White Bean Cassoulet

Ingredients:

1 Tablespoon of Olive Oil

1 1/2 Cups of Onion - Chopped

1 1/2 Cups of Carrots - Sliced

8 Ounces of Parsnip - Chopped

2 Cloves of Garlic - Minced

3 Cups of Great Northern Beans - Cooked

3/4 Cups of Vegetable Broth

1/2 Teaspoons of Thyme

1/4 Teaspoon of Salt

1/4 Teaspoon of Pepper

1 (28-ounce) Can of Diced Tomatoes - Undrained

1 Bay Leaf

1/4 Cups of Breadcrumbs

1 Ounce of Parmesan Cheese

2 Tablespoons of Butter - Melted

2 Links - Meatless Italian Sausage – Frozen, Thawed, Chopped

2 Tablespoons of Fresh Parsley - Chopped

Instructions:

Heat the oil in a large nonstick pan over medium heat.

Add the onion, carrot, the parsnip, and garlic; cover it and cook it for 5 minutes or until soft.

Place it in your slow cooker. Add the beans and the next 6 ingredients. Cover it and cook it on the low setting for 8 hours or until vegetables are soft.

Combine the breadcrumbs, the cheese, and butter in a small mixing bowl; toss it with a fork until it is moist. Stir in breadcrumb mix and sausage into the bean mixture; sprinkle it with parsley.

Nutritional Information:

Calories: 298

Total Fat: 3g

Saturated Fat: 2g

Carbohydrates: 40g

Protein: 13g

Loaded Baked Potatoes

Ingredients:

4 Small Baking Potatoes

Cooking Spray

1/8 Teaspoon of Salt

1/4 Cups of Milk

1/4 Cups of Plain Greek Yogurt

2 Ounces of Shredded Sharp Cheddar cheese - Divided

1/4 Teaspoon of Salt

1/4 Teaspoon of Pepper

1 Tablespoon of Fresh Chives - Chopped

2 Bacon Slices – Cooked, Crumbled

Instructions:

Wash the potatoes, rinse them and pat them dry with paper towels. Coat your potatoes with the spray; pierce the potatoes with a fork. Rub it with 1/8 teaspoon of salt evenly on the potatoes; place it in an oval 6-quart slow cooker. Cover it and cook it on the low setting for 8 hours or until potatoes are soft. Cool them slightly.

Cut the potatoes in half lengthwise; scoop them out put the pulp into a medium bowl, leaving a 1/8-inch-thick shell of potato. Mash up the pulp with a potato masher. Stir in the milk, the yogurt, 1/4 cups of cheese, the 1/4-teaspoon of salt, and the pepper. Microwave it at High for 1 minute.

Spoon the potato mixture evenly into the shells; sprinkle it evenly with the remaining 1/4 cups of cheese. Arrange the potato halves in the bottom of your slow cooker. Cover it and cook it on the high setting for 25 minutes. Sprinkle each potato halves with about 1/2 teaspoon of the chives and about 1 teaspoon of the bacon.

Nutritional Information:

Calories: 194

Total Fat: 12g

Saturated Fat: 1g

Carbohydrates: 15g

Protein: 15g

Chicken with Carrots and Potatoes

Ingredients:

1 3/4 Cups of Onion – Vertically Sliced

Cooking Spray

2 Cups of Baby Carrots

6 Small Round Red Potatoes - Cut into 1/4-inch Slices

1/2 Cups of Chicken Broth

1/2 Cups of Dry White Wine

1 Tablespoon of Fresh Thyme - Chopped

1 Teaspoon of Garlic - Minced

3/4 Teaspoon of Salt - Divided

1/2 Teaspoons of Pepper - Divided

1 Teaspoon of Paprika

6 (6-ounce) Chicken Thighs – Bone-In, Skinned

1 Teaspoon of Olive Oil

Chopped Fresh Thyme

Instructions:

Place the onions in a 6-quart slow cooker coated with the cooking spray; top it with carrots and the potatoes.

Combine the broth, the next 3 ingredients, 1/2 teaspoons of salt, and 1/4 teaspoon of pepper. Pour it over vegetables.

Combine the paprika, remaining 1/4 teaspoon of salt, and the remaining 1/4 teaspoon of pepper; rub it on the chicken. Heat a large nonstick pan on medium-high heat. Add the oil to a pan; swirl it to coat them. Add the chicken. Cook it for 3 minutes on each side. Arrange the chicken on top of the vegetables.

Cover it and cook it on the low setting for 3 1/2 hours. Garnish it with additional thyme.

Nutritional Information:

Calories: 229

Total Fat: 5g

Saturated Fat: 2g

Carbohydrates: 20g

Protein: 21g

Thank You!

Recipe Junkies Alert!

Sign up for Recipe Junkies FREE Newsletter today and never pay more than a buck for a brand new recipe book! Receive alerts about new recipe books before they even come out! We have many other awesome offers for subscribers eyes only! You can follow us on Facebook and Twitter as well! Come be a part of the Recipe Junkies family where recipes are our business and business is good! You are more than just a number to us and we appreciate all of our newsletter subscribers.

Recipe Junkies Alert Promo
Recipe Junkies Facebook
Recipe Junkies Twitter

Recipejunkies1@gmail.com

Check out other Amazon best sellers from the Recipe Junkie family!

CPSIA information can be obtained at www.ICGtesting.com
Printed in the USA
BVOW06s1916220216

437656BV00011B/188/P

9 781514 196236